The Life
of a Duck

Josephine Croser

MAGIC BEAN
IN - FACT

Contents

Ducks

Ducks are swimming birds found near water. They have webbed feet which help them paddle and walk across mud. Ducks eat grain, pellets, snails, worms and plenty of green leaves.

There are many kinds of duck. Some are wild, some are domestic. This book is about a kind of duck called *khaki Campbell*. 'Khaki' describes the brownish colour of their feathers. 'Campbell' was the name of the first person to breed them.

Khaki Campbells are domestic and are bred for their eggs or as garden pets. They do not fly.

The Adults

The female

The male

The adult female is called a *duck*. She has a grey bill and brown feathers which camouflage her when she sits on her nest. When the duck calls, her 'quack' is strong and clear.

The adult male is called a *drake*. He has a darker, greenish head, green bill and curly tail feathers. When the drake calls, his 'quack' sounds soft like someone with a sore throat.

4.

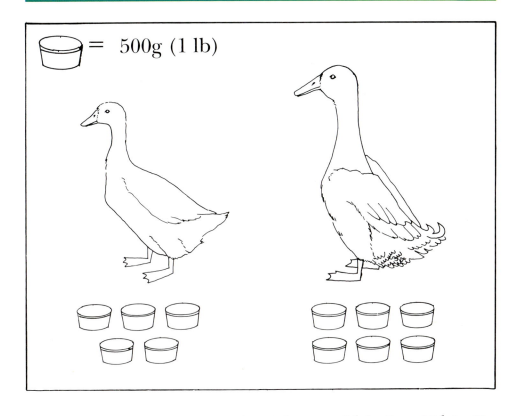

A female duck weighs about 2½ kg/5½ lb (equal to five small tubs of margarine). A drake is slightly bigger, weighing about 3 kg/6½ lb (equal to six small tubs of margarine).

A duck and drake together are called a *pair*. When they have mated, her eggs will be fertile. Ducklings can only grow from fertile eggs.

Nesting

When the duck makes a nest for her eggs, she scratches a hollow in the ground and lines it with dry leaves and twigs. She lays a new egg in the nest most mornings. When there are between twelve and eighteen eggs in the nest, she stops laying and begins to sit.

The khaki Campbell egg has a strong white shell. The pointed end comes out first as the egg is laid.

The duck sits on the nest to keep the eggs warm. Otherwise the baby birds would not grow. So whenever she leaves the nest for food, the duck covers the eggs with feathers pulled out from her own body.

If anything comes near the nest she hisses loudly to warn it to stay away.

The Embryo

Day 1

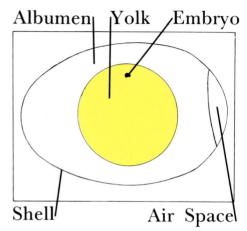

Albumen   Yolk   Embryo

Shell   Air Space

The baby bird growing inside an egg is called an *embryo*. The albumen and yolk provide the food it needs to grow. The albumen also acts as a cushion which protects the embryo if the egg is bumped. The embryo uses air from the air space at the wider end of the egg. It takes the embryo twenty-eight days to reach the hatching stage.

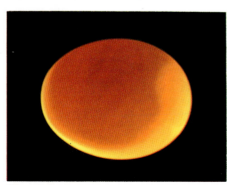

Day 8

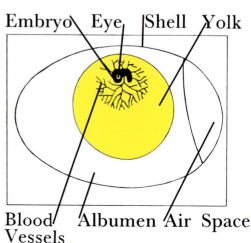

Embryo   Eye   Shell   Yolk

Blood Vessels   Albumen   Air Space

Hatching

When the ducklings are ready to hatch, they chirp and tap from inside the egg. Each duckling has a sharp scale, called an *egg tooth*, at the end of its bill (see photo p11). The duckling uses the egg tooth to break a hole in the shell from inside. This can take one or two days. The egg is now called a *pipping egg*.

During the next day, the duckling makes the hole bigger. It is such hard work that the duckling sometimes stops for a rest. Pieces of shell may fly off as the hole becomes a crack that goes almost around the egg. This can take one or two hours.

When the shell breaks open, the duckling unfolds. This takes about one or two minutes. It is damp, straggly and very tired. As each duckling hatches, the mother tosses the old shell out of the nest. The mother must be careful not to move her feet in case she crushes the half-hatched ducklings. It may be several hours before all the ducklings have hatched.

Ducklings

At first ducklings stay very close to the mother for warmth and protection. She makes gentle noises to them.

Within three to five hours of hatching, the ducklings become dry. Their soft, fluffy coats are called *down*.

After a few days, the egg tooth falls off the bill.

Day old   3 days   5 days   7 days   11 days

2 weeks   3 weeks   4 weeks   6 weeks   8 weeks

Ducklings grow quickly. They eat and drink both day and night. Some of the things they eat are small beetles, grubs, worms and bits of plant they find in the garden. They are also fed tiny crumbles — special feed made for chickens and ducklings.

When the mother duck takes her brood walking, they stay close by. She quacks loudly to call them and if one becomes lost it cries "Pip-pip-pip!" until she finds it. The ducklings seem to chatter in soft whistles when they find food.

Young Adults

Eight-week-old duck showing feathers and down   Five-month-old duck

Feathers begin to grow at three weeks. By nine weeks the young ducks are covered with feathers.

When the birds are about five months old, they are ready to mate and lay eggs. The ducklings have become ducks.

Fascinating Facts About Ducks

If a newly-hatched duckling is separated from its mother, it will follow the first moving thing it sees. It may follow a person.

Ducklings do not soil their nest. They run backwards, leave their droppings, then return to the nest.

Ducks have an oil gland near the tail. They use their bills to spread oil over their feathers. This keeps them dry in the water.

Ducks are 'sticky beaks'. If anything new is put in the garden, they crowd around to look at it.

A duck's natural lifetime is about seven years. Some ducks have been known to live longer than twelve years.

Usually, young ducks lay smaller eggs than older ducks.

Ducklings may be hatched in an incubator instead of a nest. (See back cover.)